EQUESTRIAN MONUMENTS

(Monumentos Ecuestres)

First published in Spanish by Editorial Germinal in 2011

First English version published in 2022 by

After Hours Editions
New York ◆ Kingston
afterhourseditions.com

Cover design by Eric Amling
Typesetting by Adam Robinson
in *Adobe Garamond Pro* and *Kepler Std*

ISBN: 978-1-7334082-4-0
Library of Congress Control Number: 2021940676

Luis Chaves

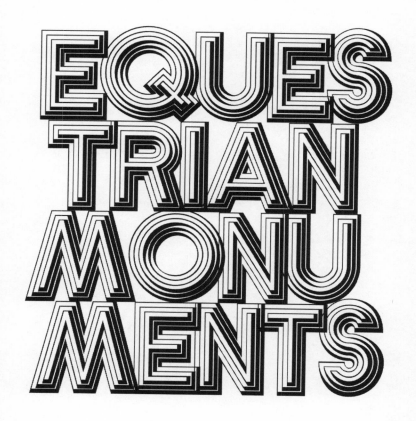

EQUESTRIAN MONUMENTS

(Monumentos Ecuestres)

Translated from the Spanish by
JULIA GUEZ & SAMANTHA ZIGHELBOIM

AFTER
HRS
editions

For Osvaldo Sauma, María Montero and César Maurel

—LC

For Edith Grossman, Ori Braun and María Montero

—JG

For Richard Howard, Sonia Zighelboim and Odette Zighelboim

—SZ

TABLE *of* CONTENTS

vii   A Note on the Translation

1   *Part One*

3   Snow/Electricity
11   Moving
19   Wyoming
21   False Fiction
25   A Wedding, One Sunday, the End of Summer
27   Sonnet
29   Santa Teresa, 2006
31   In That Photo, Fix The Pit Stains on My Shirt
37   15 Days/ Buenos Aires—Rosario—Buenos Aires
39   Equestrian Monuments (A Litany)

59   *Part Two*

61   Out Of Water
67   On a Holiday Not Everyone's Observing
71   Inventory
77   False Documentary

84   Acknowledgements

A NOTE *on the* TRANSLATION

Our task as translators has been to keep up with the hyper-caffeinated imagination of Costa Rican poet Luis Chaves, rendering each image in this remarkable collection of poetry in a way that orients the reader and provides a moment's stasis and clarity before "the waves come and the waves erase it."

The questions, concerns and themes Chaves centers in this collection range from the quotidian to the metaphysical. In *Equestrian Monuments,* dialogue from *The Exorcist* co-exists with lines from the Latin prayer "Kyrie eleison." The stately figure of a former president, Leon Cortés, is counterbalanced by a cast of mock-heroic characters. The intersections are uncanny, sometimes hilarious, often sad and unsettling.

Sweeping statements about entire generations, continents and genres find a basis in the most intimate details of domestic life. The poems are inventive and playful, irreverent and, at the same time, full of grace. Chaves moves seamlessly between high- and low- registers. That is also true for the way he plays with scale, often rendering the most complex thoughts and feelings with the simplest diction:

> La maleza crece
> cuando dejamos de mirar.
> Los años se acumulan
> mientras nos ocupamos de la maleza.
> Aprender esto nos tomó
> más tiempo del que hubiéramos querido.

We've worked hard to maintain a similar syntax and style, trying to capture the ease, colloquialism and play of the Spanish without losing any depth or seriousness in this translation into English.

> The weeds grow
> when we're not watching them.
> Years accumulate
> while we worry about the weeds.
> Learning this took
> longer than we would have liked.

Monumentos Ecuestres was a gift, given to Guez the first time she and Chaves met for Imperial and espresso at the Hotel Costa Rica, when they were sitting on the patio across from the Teatro Nacional before heading to the Librería Duluoz nearby. Guez was in the country on a year-long grant from The Fulbright Commission. This allowed her to spend half of her time in Vargas Arraya where she and her fiancée rented a small white-walled room in a guest house. So close to the Universidad de Costa Rica in San Pedro, she wasn't far from some of the presses—Lanzallamas, Perro Azul, Espiral and Germinal—whose work she was there to research.

In and around the capital, Guez reveled in as many readings, salons and festivals as she could, then resolved to spend the rest of her time living in the small town of Delicias where, half-way up a massive hill, she rented the second story of a house overlooking the Gulf of Nicoya. It was there that she made the first attempt to translate *Equestrian Monuments* on her own. She would tinker with individual words and phrases for weeks and months.

The project of successfully re-creating the experience of reading Luis Chaves really began to come together when, over drinks and tacos at Mercadito in New York City's East Village, Guez invited Zighelboim into a conversation about co-translating the collection together.

We first met at Columbia University's School of the Arts. The project of preparing for the annual thesis reading in the spring of 2010 gave us a window into what we were both reading, writing and translating at the time and the extent to which we could trust one another's eye and ear. That small-scale collaboration hinted at the kind of ambition, humor, integrity, persistence and care that would allow us to do some extraordinary work together on a larger-scale project like this one.

After that drink at Mercadito, we would meet at one of our two apartments (or a coffee shop halfway between) almost every week for the next five years to translate the manuscript. In the beginning, our aim was simply to be generative. We wanted to come up with as many counterfactuals as we could, so we would list all our options out, each separated by a backslash, without much editorializing. After trimming down some of these initial solutions, the goal was to narrow the field of our focus. If something didn't work—even if it was completely accurate, and even if we couldn't put our finger on why it didn't attain what Walter Lowrie's translation of Kierkegaard called a "lyrical validity" in English—it was removed from the list we had bracketed-out before. At this point, we were literally halving the size of our drafts.

We then aimed to create enough distance between ourselves and the text, enough time and space to be able to come back and see everything with new eyes. Sometimes a few minutes—to prepare another gourd of mate or go outside for a cigarette—would be sufficient. Other days, we would need to take a few hours off—to pick up a bottle of wine for dinner, eat, drink, then begin again. Several weeks and months (and eventually, years) would pass between drafts of the trickiest poems in the collection.

Finally, our aim was to dilate moments in the text that still didn't sound right to us. Unsatisfied with the options we had generated so far, we gave ourselves greater permission vis-à-vis inserting or eliding something in the English to protect the flow of a line (without

altering its meaning and, likely, only adding to its plausibility). "The waves come and the waves erase it" is one example. We repeated the word "waves" to maintain the lilt of the phrase "y las olas vienen y la borran" and to convey the sense of ritual and repetition that is at the heart of this particular poem. Raindrops were "veining" the window. The crickets "came on" after "the fog cleared." And "the sky's own white stone path" was chosen in lieu of cloud-like rolling stones: every other way we attempted to translate that phrase up to this point felt clichéd, distracting and allusive in a way the Spanish didn't mean to be. In the end, everything we had pressure-tested for months still pleased us.

In this collaboration, our commitment to question every choice we have made, to consider and reconsider everything almost compulsively, inclined us to spend years talking about how to render particular words and references in ways that neither one of us could have come up with on our own.

In our translation then, "provincia" has become "suburb" and "clonazepam" is "Klonopin." These departures are straightforward enough and very much serve the text and the audience encountering this collection for the first time in English. Where a literal translation would require us to consider using language that is difficult if not impossible to separate from a history of able-ism and homophobia in our culture, we depart further. "Un cojo" included in the phrase "un cojo que arrastra su pierna muerta por la arena del Pacifico" becomes "the man with a limp who drags his leg through the sand of the Pacific." To refer to the genderqueer figure in the title-poem, we have chosen to render "travesti" as "drag queen." Where Chaves uses the word "obesidad," we have chosen to use "fatness." "Abuela" is still "abuela." "Gringos" are still "gringos." And "La Virgen Criolla" is still "La Virgen Criolla." There are mystical, slippery and strange references in the original and we attempt to make them feel the same way in our translation: a necessary strangeness.

—Julia Guez and Samantha Zighelboim
New York City, 2021

The time of minor poets is coming. Good-bye Whitman,
Dickinson, Frost. Welcome you whose fame will never
reach beyond your closest family, and perhaps one or
two good friends gathered after dinner over a jug of
fierce red wine... while the children are falling asleep
and complaining about the noise you're making as you
rummage through the closets for your old poems,
afraid your wife might've thrown them out with last
spring's cleaning.

It's snowing, says someone who has peeked into the
dark night, and then he, too, turns towards you as you
prepare yourself to read, in a manner somewhat
theatrical and with a face turning red, the long
rambling love poem whose final stanza (unknown to
you) is hopelessly missing.

(After Aleksander Ristovic)

— Charles Simic,
The World Doesn't End: Prose Poems.
(New York, Harcourt Brace, 1989)

Part **ONE**

EQUES
TRIAN
MONU
MENTS

LA NIEVE, LA ELECTRICIDAD

La ropa tendida
y esas nubes.

Hay un perro nuevo,
me sigue a todas partes
aquí está debajo de la mesa,
cuando llueve con truenos
se clava al piso y no lo mueve nadie.

La casa está igual
menos la cocina,
la ampliamos botando la pared de atrás.
Ahora es más moderna,
tiene mostrador de granito
como en las revistas que mandaste,
cuando mandabas cosas.

Pusimos piedras blancas en el jardín,
hacen camino hasta la puerta.
Antes de llover
o cuando ya casi oscureció
entra el olor de la albahaca.
Eso tampoco ha cambiado,
todos los días
de todos los años,
esté quién esté,
ese aroma entra apenas
a la parte de la casa

SNOW/ELECTRICITY

Clothes out to dry
and those clouds.

There's a new dog
who follows me everywhere
I go. He is here now,
under the table. When it's storming
he flattens himself onto the floor
and will not be moved.

The house is the same
except for the kitchen,
which we opened up some
by knocking out the back wall.
It's more modern now;
it has granite countertops
like the ones in those magazines you sent
back when you used to send me things.

We put small white stones in the garden,
forming a path to the door.
At dusk or before
it rains, the smell of basil.
This hasn't changed either.
Year in and year out,
regardless of who's around,
the same scent faintly
enters this part of the house

que da al jardín
como siguiendo el camino de piedras.

Entra la albahaca
luego llueve
u oscurece.

Tenemos la misma tele
aunque parezca mentira.
Anoche, por cierto,
mientras pensaba en otra cosa
en un programa pasaban
la imagen de unas torres enormes
clavadas en campos verdes
para sacar electricidad del viento.
Todas en fila, formadas,
las hélices enormes y lentas
giraban a destiempo,
perdían la sincronización.

Entonces dejé la otra cosa
y pensé en eso
un buen rato:
cómo sería ir ahí,
el silencio mecánico talvez
al pie de una torre.
Luego me quedé dormido
.

Afuera pasan las nubes
en formación,
las piedras del cielo parecen,
piedras rodantes.

that overlooks the garden
as if it's following the stone path.

The basil
then the rain
or the dusking.

Believe it or not
we still have the same TV.
Last night, there was this show
on. While I was thinking about something
else entirely, an enormous wind farm—
turbines staked into green
fields—flickered across the screen.
They were all in a row, in formation;
the blades, enormous and slow,
harnessing electricity from the wind.
They turned out of time,
losing synchronization.

So I forget about whatever else I am thinking
and instead think of this for a while:
what it would be like to go there,
to the foot of a windmill—
a mechanical silence, perhaps.
Then I fall asleep.

Outside the clouds arrange
themselves in a kind of formation.
Like the sky's own white stone path
in motion.

Va a llover
y tengo ropa tendida.
Los truenos son el sonido
de la electricidad.
Te dejo esa frase de revista
mientras el perro tiembla,
atornillado al piso.

Puede ser tu lugar
donde están esas torres,
no entendí mucho
era el canal alemán o el francés,
a mí me suenan igual.
Unas praderas extensas,
parches verdes
de gramíneas diferentes
como corrientes de agua
o manchas de diesel
que se juntan
sin mezclarse.

Cómo será su casa,
la ruta que lleva a la puerta,
la ropa secándose en un balcón.
En la tele veo programas de lugares y viajes
como el de anoche
o uno con gente rodeada de blanco
hundida hasta las rodillas.
Luego el mismo lugar sin gente,
sin otro sonido que el tic tac interno,
el que no viene del televisor.

It's going to rain
and I have clothes drying on the line.
Thunder is the sound of electricity.
I leave you with this phrase from a magazine
while the dog trembles,
flattening himself on the floor.

Maybe you live where
those windmills are.
I couldn't understand much—
it was the German or French channel—
all sounds the same to me.
Lawn-like stretches,
green patches
of different kinds of grasses
like seams in a slow moving river
or striations of color
in a slick of diesel
that come together
without ever mixing.

I wonder what your house is like—
the path leading to your front door,
clothes drying on a balcony.
On TV I watch shows about travel
like the one on last night
with people buried up to
their knees in snow somewhere.
Then the same place without any people,
without any other sound but the internal tick-tack
which isn't coming from the television.

Daban ganas de estar ahí.
La nieve en la tele,
detrás de la electricidad,
me pregunto cosas,
tu lugar, qué pensarás
antes de que llueva
o anochezca,
cosas así pienso
hasta que me duermo.
Me sigue el perro
pero se queda afuera,
al pie de la puerta.
No entra a este sueño
como de aspas gigantes
en cámara lenta,
la nieve al otro lado
de la electricidad.
Huele a albahaca,
es de noche
o va a llover.
Cuánto pesarán,
me pregunto,
sacando la mano
por el balcón de tu casa,
los copos,
los copos de nieve,
cuánto duran en la mano.

Behind a wall of electricity,
the snow on TV
makes me want to be there.
I wonder about your home, what you're thinking
before it rains
or grows dark.
This is the sort of thing I think about
until I fall asleep.

The dog follows me around
but stays outside
on the stoop.
He doesn't appear in this dream
like the gigantic blades
moving in slow motion,
the snow on the other side
of the electricity.

The air smells of basil.
It's night
or it's going to rain.

How much does snow weigh,
I ask myself,
reaching over the balcony at your house;
how long can a snowflake last in my hands.

MUDANZAS

1.
Si vieras.
Dos semanas de temporal
borraron la huella ocre
de las macetas.

Revuelta en la lavadora,
ropa blanca y de color.

Una casa reducida a cajas de cartón
la tarde que gira sobre el eje de la lluvia.
El mentolado falso
de un Derby suave + una Halls.

Ese color de la plasticina
cuando se mezclan todas las barras.

2.
El mundo da tantas vueltas
que parece no moverse.
Pensé decirlo
pero preferí, de copiloto,
verte manejar en círculos
por el estacionamiento.

MOVING

1.
Picture this:
Ochre rings from all
the flower pots washed
away by two weeks of rain.

The whites and darks mix
in the same washing machine.

A house reduced to cardboard boxes.
The afternoon spinning on the rain's axis.
The menthol
of a Derby Light + a Halls.

The color plasticine bars make
when they've been kneaded together.

2.
The world is turning so fast
it appears to be standing still.
I thought about saying so
but, as your copilot, preferred
to watch you circle
the parking lot.

3.
Las hormigas vinieron
en las cajas de la mudanza.
El apartamento nuevo
empieza a parecer una casa.
De otro, pero una casa.

4.
En el apartamento nuevo,
el albañil pica la pared buscando
dónde está la fuga de agua.

No es desorden lo que se ve,
es un orden disparejo.

Bolsas plásticas,
cartones con cursiva en pilot
Cocina / libros / baño
Si otro, en este momento, entrara,
no sabría si alguien llega o se va.

5.
Envuelto en la nicotina
de la inmovilidad,
se ablanda el cerebro
y se endurece el corazón.

Sin camisa me veo más viejo,
pensé decirlo pero preferí
recordar la vez que fui tu copiloto
y manejabas en círculos
por el estacionamiento.

3.
Ants came in
the moving boxes.
The new apartment
begins to feel more like a home.
One belonging to someone else, but still—a home.

4.
In the new apartment,
the handyman hollows out a wall
searching for the leak.
This isn't disorder per se,
but order of another kind.

Plastic bags, Sharpie
on boxes, in cursive:
kitchen/books/bathroom.
If someone else were to walk in at this moment,
they wouldn't know if we were moving in or out.

5.
Inert, enveloped
in nicotine,
the brain goes soft;
the heart hardens.

I look older without a shirt on.
I thought about saying so, but preferred
to remember the time I was
your copilot as you kept
circling the lot.

6.
Francisca, silenciosa,
se mueve por cada ambiente.
Para allá con la escoba,
para acá con el balde.
Dentro de esa boca,
siempre cerrada,
brilla un diente de oro.

7.
Una pausa que amenaza
con convertirse en otra cosa.
La ropa sin tender,
el gusto del falso mentol,
el espacio libre
donde finalmente parqueaste.

8.
Alrededor de latas de cerveza,
los amigos discutían
cuánto dura la juventud.
Pensaste en voz alta
"qué me importa, si nunca fui joven".

Luego se agitó el borrador de la niebla.
Luego irrumpieron los grillos.

9.
Aquí tendría que ir una frase decisiva
pero se destiñe la camiseta

6.
Without a sound, Francisca
moves through each space—
here with the bucket,
there with the broom—
inside her mouth,
always closed,
the glint of a gold tooth.

7.
A pause that threatens to become
something else entirely.

Clothes we haven't unpacked,
the taste of menthol,
that spot where
you finally parked the car.

8.
Over a few rounds
some friends argue about
how long we can keep calling ourselves young.
What does it matter,
you think aloud,
if I was never young to begin with.

Then the fog cleared. Then
the crickets came on.

9.
Here's where a decisive phrase should go
but the t-shirt I was wearing

de la tarde que hablábamos
mientras crecía el pasto
y sin darte cuenta
usabas mis muletillas
cada seis palabras.

Lo que no se va a secar,
lo que brilla sin elección,
un período equivocado para la mudanza,
el cerebro: masa de plasticina,
el corazón: dos puertas de carro
que sólo saben cerrarse.

10.
Debajo de esto hay una canción,
aunque no se escucha ni se ve.

Las promesas de la casa nueva
quedaron en la casa vieja.

Del temporal va quedando ese color
 de todas las barras de plasticina
que se mezclan se mezclan,
el martilleo que silencia
la tenacidad de una fuga,
esas gotas de lluvia
como las venas de la ventana.
Y el canto de los grillos
crece como otra niebla.
Debajo de esto hay algo mejor.

that afternoon fades
while the grass grows,
and without realizing it,
every other word,
you begin to use some of my own verbal tics.

What in this weather will never dry;
what shines whether we like it or not;
the wrong time of year to move—
the brain: a lump of plasticine,
the heart: two car doors
that only know how to close.

10.
Underneath all of this there's a song,
even if it can't be seen or heard.

The promise of a new house
stayed behind in the old one.

What remains of the rainy season is a blend
of all the plasticine bars—
what will be kneaded together is kneaded
together, hammering that quiets
the tenacity of a leak,
raindrops
veining the window.
And the crickets' song
swelling like another fog.
Underneath all of this there is something better.

WYOMING

Falta el inicio
pero es lo de menos:
huele a gas y una tarde
por la ventana del bus:
el rótulo de gaseosa Goliat.

Inquieto en el cielo raso,
el reflejo del reloj.

Las faldas dentro del calzoncillo,
la constelación de hormigas
suspendidas dentro de la botella de miel.

Hasta aquí va todo bien,
ahora la parte difícil,
viene la fuerza de gravedad,
el adormecimiento.

Algo es seguro:
sopla un viento helado
en, digamos, Bahía Blanca.
Mudo el manto de escarcha
sobre la tierra plana de Wyoming.

WYOMING

There is no beginning
but that's the least of our concerns:
one afternoon, the reek of gasoline
and an ad for Goliat soda
seen through the window of this bus.

The watch's reflection
flickers against the still sky.

The hem of a skirt
bunched up in a pair of panties,
a constellation of ants
suspended in a jar of honey.

All is well until this point,
now for the hard part:
drowsiness
comes on with the force of gravity.

This much is certain:
a cold wind blows
in, say, Bahía Blanca.
Mute is the mantle of frost
over the flatlands of Wyoming.

FALSA FICCIÓN

Pero hay un intento de reconstrucción
con pocos elementos,
una sombra que sale de escena,
el olor a laca y el rótulo
—pero es otro— de gaseosa Goliat
atrapado con el rabo del ojo
desde el bus que se adentra
en la masa maleable
de julio del 2004.
El de aquel invierno sudaca
sin calefacción.

Se cuenta hasta diez
con los dedos,
empezando por el meñique
 o el pulgar.
No es lo mismo aunque parece,
ni es lo mismo, a las 3 a.m.,
afuera de la cantina, parqueado,
nuestro carro con el árbol de navidad
atado al techo.

Aquí pasó agua debajo del puente,
huimos de un lugar
que apestaba a World Music,
que hedía a New Age.
Aquí no hay cuatro estaciones:
por encima de la línea del Ecuador

FALSE FICTION

Here's an attempt at reconstructing
everything with only a few elements:
a shadow leaving the stage,
the smell of lacquer and the ad
—not the same one—for Goliat soda
caught out of the corner of my eye
from this bus entering into
the kneadable dough
of July, 2004.
The one from that South American winter
when we didn't have heat.

You count to ten
on your fingers,
beginning with the pinky
or the thumb.
It's not the same although it would seem to be,
nor is it the same, at 3am,
outside the bar, parked, our car
the one with the Christmas tree tied on
to the roof.

Here's where it was all water under the bridge,
when we abandoned a place
saturated with World Music,
reeking of New Age.
There aren't four seasons here:
above the equator,

por debajo de la línea de flotación.
Nueve meses de lluvia
nos han enseñado a nadar
a consumirnos de cabeza,
en el confort del verso libre.

Un ejemplo,
por toda la casa me siguen
mi hija, la gata y la perra.
Son mi sombra buena.

Huele a gas también,
y trabajan a full los aleros.
El metrónomo del goteo

El año va dando señales:
esto casi mejora,
la perra se enrosca
con la calma de la evolución.
Es fácil saberlo,
para terminar lo que falta
no nos necesitan.

above the waterline.
Nine months of rain
have taught us to swim,
to lose ourselves—
in the comfort of free verse.
For example, all over the house
I am followed
by my daughter, the cat and the dog.
They are my good shadows.

It smells of gas again,
and the eaves are working overtime.
The metronome of that slow drip
divides the day into fractions.

The year goes on giving us signs:
this almost gets better.
The dog curls up
with evolutionary calm.

It's easy enough to see,
they don't need us
to figure out the rest.

UNA BODA, UN DOMINGO, EL FIN DEL VERANO

A las 11 a.m., con los primeros en llegar, se descorchará la botella inaugural (a lo largo del día el arco democrático del vino cubrirá desde cosechas 2004 hasta cajas de tetrabrik). A las 11 p.m., ya en su casa, demasiado cerca del lunes, herido de gravedad por *la bala lenta del alcohol*, el último en haberse ido repasará, en diapositivas mentales, el primer domingo de marzo: el sol trazando su línea de 180 grados en cámara lenta; la multiplicación del pan y las reses; la montaña de zapatos revueltos en la entrada de la casa; la imagen de alguien, mitad del cuerpo dentro de la refri, buceando por cervezas; un guiso prodigioso preparado con ingredientes de una galaxia muy lejana; el recuerdo de los extensos y turbadores segundos en que sostuvo contacto visual con un perro; y el efecto dominó de la reproducción materializado en aquellas niñas que se bañan chingas en la piscina.

A WEDDING, ONE SUNDAY, THE END OF SUMMER

At 11 in the morning, as the first few guests arrive, the inaugural bottle of wine will be uncorked. Over the course of the day, drinking's democratic arc will range from 2004's old vine varietals to box wine. 11 at night, back at your house, Monday altogether too close and here we are, seriously wounded by alcohol's slow-moving bullet. Those of us who've yet to leave will now replay the first Sunday of March in a slideshow of our minds' own making: the sun in slow-motion, tracing its 180° sweep across the sky; brisket and bread multiplying; a pile of shoes in a mess by the front door; the image of someone's body half submerged inside the fridge, fumbling for more beer; a prodigious stew prepared with ingredients that may as well be from another galaxy; a flashback to those vast and troubling seconds you were able to keep unbroken eye contact with the dog; and the undeniable domino effect of being alive made real by our children here, swimming naked in the pool.

SONETO

Un 1o de enero, de madrugada, aterrizando en Ezeiza y, visto desde la ventana, el conejo o liebre que corría al lado del avión. Saltaba del asfalto a la gramilla y otra vez al asfalto de la pista, tratando de llevar el paso de aquella máquina gigante.

SONNET

On January 1, landing at Ezeiza at dawn, a rabbit or maybe a hare ran alongside the plane. Bounding from the asphalt to the grass and back again to the asphalt, it strained to keep up with the gigantic machine on the tarmac.

PLAYA SANTA TERESA, 2006

Unos días con sus noches en Malpaís y Santa Teresa. Vi los pelícanos, los cocos asesinos, vi pizotes, ballenas, iguanas, garzas y unos peces azules minúsculos y fosforescentes nadando en las pozas que se forman en las rocas cuando baja la marea. También las gaviotas que nos seguían en la terraza del ferry para que las alimentáramos con snacks ultraquímicos. Vi amigos, vi a los hijos de los amigos. Vi a los amigos y a los hijos de los amigos encender una fogata en la noche y así cumplir con ese ritual que nos acompaña desde no sabemos cuándo. Vi el mar cada noche antes de dormirme y lo vi también cada mañana al despertarme. Vi una cometa multicolor inmóvil contra el cielo limpio, vi que la cuerda invisible que la sostenía llegaba hasta mis manos. Vi caricacos de todos los tamaños rodeándome mientras meaba en la arena. Vi, en el fondo de la mochila, el lomo de la novela de Dos Passos que ni siquiera llegué a abrir. Vi los objetos que el mar deposita en la orilla: una piedra con forma de cassette, una rama con forma de linterna, una lata de birra con forma de lata de birra. Una tarde cerré los ojos y vi muchos viajes ya borrosos del pasado e imaginé paseos futuros en esta misma costa. Es así, la vida se puede reducir a una lista breve.

SANTA TERESA, 2006

A few days in Malpaís and Santa Teresa. I saw the pelicans, the threat of falling coconuts, I saw coatis, whales, iguanas, herons and some fish—blue, miniscule and phosphorescent—swimming in pools that form among the rocks at low-tide. Also the seagulls who followed us onto the deck of the ferry so that we'd feed them highly-processed snacks. I saw friends, I saw friends' children. I saw friends and friends' children light a bonfire in the night and fulfill this ritual that's been with us for who knows how long. I saw the ocean each night before I'd fall asleep and I saw it each morning when I'd wake up. I saw a multi-colored comet, flickering against the clean sky, I saw the invisible string that seemed to sustain it reach almost to my own hands. I saw hermit crabs of all sizes surrounding me while I pissed on the sand. I saw, in the bottom of my backpack, the spine of a Dos Passos novel I hadn't gotten around to opening. I saw objects the sea deposits on the shore: a stone in the shape of a cassette tape, a branch in the shape of a lantern, a beer can in the shape of a beer can. One afternoon I closed my eyes and saw the blur of so many past trips, imagining future visits to this very coast. This is how it is. Life can be pared down to a very short list.

EN LA FOTO, BORRAME
EL ARCO DE SUDOR DE LA CAMISA

Alguien va a soñar con esto.
La cabeza en la segunda casa,
el cuerpo en una barra, al centro,
equidistante de dos gringos.

Íbamos para otra parte
hasta que sonó el despertador
de la realidad:
"borrame —me dice— en la foto
el arco de sudor de la camisa".

El cambio climático
es escuchar, al paso,
el hit del verano en invierno.
Una palabra como antirretrovirales
en un poema aspiracional.

El veneno paralizador de la edad.
Los días, una sucesión perfecta
de prueba y error.

Aquellas bengalas al final
de las manos de ocho años,
estiradas a lo alto
contra una noche de estrellas.
El perro de la memoria
en la casa de abuela Belén,

IN THAT PHOTO, FIX
THE PIT STAINS ON MY SHIRT

Someone's going to dream about this.
Head in the second house, the body
centered: a brick, a bar,
equidistant from two gringos.

We were about to go somewhere else
when an alarm began to signal
another reality:
"In that photo"—it tells me— "fix
the pit stains on my shirt."

Climate change is listening
to summer's hit song
mid-winter.
A word like "antiretroviral"
in even the most visionary poem.

The paralyzing venom of age.
The days, a perfect succession
of trial and error.

Those flares at the end
of eight year-old hands
gesturing toward a star-filled sky.
In my memory of abuela Belén's house—

Puntarenas 1973,
oliéndonos la entrepierna
(un recuerdo talvez falso),
y el sonido, atrás, de un tren
invisible como los grillos.

Queda siempre la ciencia
y el taladro de los zancudos
penetrando el sueño
de una noche de calor.
Las banderas y pitos
de la socialdemocracia,
el Datsun 120Y
desde donde asomabas
medio cuerpo por la ventana.

Una taza de café
en la que se sumerge
el pan con margarina.
Las mini agujas de la garúa,
la sensación de   .

Allí pasan las nubes
en formación,
las piedras del cielo
sobre nuestras cabezas.
A lo lejos y al pasar,
hélices gigantes y lentas
pierden la sincronización.

Puntarenas 1973—
the dog sniffs our crotches
(maybe I'm remembering this all wrong)
and at the same time the sound of a train
invisible as the crickets.

If nothing else, there's still science
and the drilling of mosquitos
upsetting another sweaty night's sleep.
Social democracy—the rallying,
the flags, you
leaning half your body out
of that Datsun 120Y.

Margarine on a piece of toast
dunked in a cup of coffee.
The drizzle like infinitesimal pinpricks,
the sensation of _____.

That's where the clouds arrange
themselves in formation,
the sky's own stone path
in motion above our heads.
Farther on, blades
enormous and slow
lose their synchronization.

Entonces, había que volver
por la ruta larga.
Alguno, fuiste vos creo,
tarareaba la canción
saltándose palabras que
agregábamos sin hablar,
y el olor a pollo asado
avanzaba en oleadas
desde las filas de atrás.

¿Cuánto falta?
pregunta el niño de la mente
y la bengala entra, en cámara lenta,
a la noche de estrellas
hasta consumirse.

Ahora se ven unas luces. Allá.
¿Las ves?

We had to take the long way back.
Someone was humming
a song—was it you?
I think it was you—
unlearning the lyrics
because we'd made up our own,
and from the backseat,
the smell of rotisserie chicken
came on in waves.

In my mind, the child asks
how much longer?
And in slow motion, the flare
darts across the sky until
it's swallowed by the star-filled night.

You can see a few lights now.
There.
See them?

15 DÍAS/BUENOS AIRES— ROSARIO—BUENOS AIRES

Ana, Nacho, Carlos, Fabián, Juan, Francisco, Ivana, Daniel, Martín, Cecilia, Valentín, Cristian, Fernanda, Simón, Damián, Pablo, Gilda, Damián, Marina, Marcela, Cecilia, Paula, Daniel, Irene, Horacio, Gabriela, Mariajosé, Santiago, Daniel, Jeymer, Eric, Elena, Agustina, Ana Luisa, Pedro, Inés, Guadalupe, Ana, Martín, Inés, Ana Laura, Solana, Leandro, Marcela, Martín, Karina, Gustavo, Milton, Julia, Ramiro, Natalia, Bárbara.

15 DAYS / BUENOS AIRES—ROSARIO—BUENOS AIRES

Ana, Nacho, Carlos, Fabian, Juan, Francisco, Ivana,
Daniel, Martín, Cecilia, Valentín, Cristian, Fernanda,
Simon, Damian, Pablo, Gilda, Damian, Marina,
Marcela, Cecilia, Paula, Daniel, Irene, Horacio,
Gabriela, Mariajosé, Santiago, Daniel, Jeymer, Eric,
Elena, Agustina, Ana Luisa, Pedro, Inés, Guadalupe,
Ana, Martin, Inés, Ana Laura, Solana, Leandro,
Marcela, Martin, Karina, Gustavo, Milton, Julia,
Ramiro, Natalia, Barbara.

MONUMENTOS ECUESTRES
(UNA LETANÍA)

Fotos mal enfocadas
frente a monumentos ecuestres.

La bruma de la droga,
anécdotas de bajo impacto
y pasajes de películas mal dobladas

Con esto llegamos a los 40,
 no seamos malagradecidos,
podría ser peor.

**

Aquel año terminando
en el mes de los pericos
que a nadie dejaban dormir
con sus chillidos dementes.

Fecha cuando bajamos los brazos
creyendo que los subíamos.

**

Un brazo, el fragmento de un brazo
congelado en el borde izquierdo:
la foto donde posamos como turistas
en la ciudad más fea del mundo.

EQUESTRIAN MONUMENTS
(A LITANY)

Out-of-focus photographs
in front of equestrian monuments.

The fog of the drug,
low-impact anecdotes,
scenes from badly dubbed films.

With this we arrive at our 40s.
We shouldn't be ungrateful.
It could be worse.

**

The year ending
with the month of parakeets
who didn't let anyone sleep
with their demented squawking.

The day we lowered our arms
believing we were raising them.

**

An arm, a fragment of an arm
congealed on the left margin:
the photograph in which we're posing like tourists
in the ugliest city in the world.

La extremidad salida de cuadro
avanzando hacia un destino
sin valor para la Historia.
Esa foto,
la mecánica de la sonrisa activada
por la señal del desconocido que la tomó.

**

La poesía es la voz del recuerdo.
Aquí, sin embargo, se habla del futuro.
No del abstracto, no de la posteridad:
en media hora saldremos de esta oficina
conscientes de que el mes entrante,
como los últimos cuarenta y nueve,
tampoco podremos renunciar.

**

Para no pensar en lo inminente e
speculemos sobre el destino
del compañero de primaria
que forraba sus cuadernos de rosado.
O seamos prácticos
y calculemos los impuestos.

**

Dios guarde, piensa.
Diusguardi, dice.

An extremity outside the frame
pointing towards a place
without historical value.
That photograph,
the mechanics of a smile set in motion
by a signal from the stranger who was taking it.

**

Poetry is the voice of memory.
Here, however, we speak of the future.
Not of the abstract, not of posterity:
in half an hour, we'll be leaving this office
conscious that, in the coming month—
same as the last forty-nine—
we can't resign.

**

To keep from dwelling on the imminent
let's speculate about the fate
of a friend from elementary school
who always covered his notebooks in pink.
Or to be practical,
let's calculate our taxes.

**

May God keep you, she thinks.
Blessings, she says.

**

Cada cuatro meses,
cual chequeo técnico,
mamá pregunta si soy gay.

**

Hijo (abandonando la mesa): Nos vemos mañana
Madre (entre dientes): Si Dios quiere.

**

Vacaciones del 91,
turno vespertino
digitando el catálogo
de copias piratas.
El exorcista en repeat por semanas
hasta aprender de memoria los diálogos
de los que, 15 años después, nada queda.

El ejercicio inútil
de unas vacaciones.
La crisis de los 40
a los 22.

**

La maleza crece
cuando dejamos de mirar.
Los años se acumulan

**

Every four months,
like a technical inspection,
Mom asks if I'm gay.

**

Son (leaving the table): See you tomorrow.
Mother (under her breath): God willing, yes.

**

Vacation of '91,
evening shift
downloading the catalog
of bootlegs.
The Exorcist on repeat for weeks
to commit the dialogue to memory:
15 years later, nothing remains.

The useless exercise
of a vacation.
The crisis of 40
at 22.

**

The weeds grow
when we're not watching them.
Years accumulate

mientras nos ocupamos de la maleza.
Aprender esto nos tomó
más tiempo del que hubiéramos querido.

**

– "Nos vemos mañana".
– "Dios primero", me corrige.

**

Del sol, otra vez superado
por rotación y traslación,
quedan escasos minutos de luz naranja
 favoreciendo las siluetas
de los viejos inmóviles del parque.

Es así o es lo que veo a través
del filtro atenuante
de 10 mg de clonazepán.

**

La bruma de la droga,
anécdotas de bajo impacto
y pasajes de películas mal dobladas.

A esa hora de la mañana
en que a los travestis
les crece la barba.

while we worry about the weeds.
Learning this took
longer than we would have liked.

**

"See you tomorrow."
She corrects me, "God willing, yes."

**

From the sun, surpassed again
by rotation and refraction,
a few minutes of orange light are left
flattering the silhouettes
of the park's elderly, unmoving.

This is how it is or this is how I see it through
the extenuating filter
of 10 mg of Klonopin.

**

The fog of the drug,
low-impact anecdotes,
scenes from badly dubbed films.

At that hour of the morning
when drag queens begin
to grow beards.

**

Vicios que explican la mirada vidriosa
de quien vio al otro que,
en una zona libre de la mesa,
ocupada por electrodomésticos robados,
planchaba primero billetes viejos
para después, minucioso,
restaurarlos con cinta scotch.

**

Jorge (jardinero) poda la maleza.
–Nos vemos mañana.
–Que Dios lo acompañe.

**

Casa de los padres
un domingo de gordura
(pantalón desabotonado),
toda idea es pecado capital
en el sofá frente a la tele.
Pasan la peli de uno
con corazón de mandril.
O eso, desde niño, le hicieron creer.

El músculo débil
sustituido por una fantasía.

**

**

Vices explain the glassy stare
of someone who saw somebody
else ironing the old bills first
on a table otherwise
occupied by stolen appliances
to later, meticulously,
restore them with Scotch tape.

**

Jorge (the gardener) is weeding.
"See you tomorrow."
"God be with you."

**

Parents' house,
a gluttonous Sunday
(pants unbuttoned),
every idea is a capital sin
on the sofa in front of the TV.
They show the movie about someone
with the heart of a baboon.
Or, since childhood, that's what they made him
believe.

The weak muscle
substituted by a fantasy.

**

Entregado a la interrupción,
escribe esto:
"sobre el bar donde hubo alegría
construyeron la catedral
de todo lo que no me pertenece".

**

Entregado a la interrupción
recita esto:
"Kyrie, rex genitor ingenite,
vera essentia, eleyson".

**

Antes me preocupaba la muerte,
ahora el sobrepeso.
El cerebro: órgano autónomo
seducido por la frivolidad.

**

Dato estadístico:
"tengo fotos que antes tuvimos".
Un corazón débil. Sin fantasía.

**

Años y años,
horas y horas

Succumbing to the interruption,
he writes this:
"Above the bar where joy had been
they built a cathedral
out of everything that doesn't belong to me."

**

Succumbing to the interruption,
he recites this:
"Kyrie, rex genitor ingenite,
vera essentia, eleyson."

**

Before I'd worry about death;
now, weight gain.
The brain: autonomous organ
seduced by frivolity.

**

Statistic:
"I have photographs that used to be ours."
A weak heart. No fantasy.

**

Years and years,
hours and hours

dedicadas a ejercitar el cerebro
que responde sólo a lo superficial.

Un órgano autónomo
dicta el dolor
—no metafórico— de corazón.

**

En mi cabeza hay una persona diminuta que pica
piedras, también un cojo que arrastra su pierna muerta
por la arena del Pacífico y la huella que va dejando
parece la escritura de uno que te hizo daño, y las olas
vienen y la borran.

**

Conversaciones en las que no puede participar.

Pilas de libros pendientes.

Llaveros con focos inútiles.

El camino de hormigas parece una grieta en la pared.

Escribir en el propio antebrazo con el borde filoso de
la uña
cortada a diente.

Súper: arroz, mostaza, pasta de dientes, cinta scotch,
acetaminofén.

dedicated to exercising the brain
which responds solely to the superficial.

An autonomous organ
dictates the heart's
—not at all metaphorical—ache.

**

In my head there's a homunculus who skips stones
and also a man with a limp who drags his leg through
the sand of the Pacific such that the trail he's leaving
behind looks like the handwriting of someone who's
hurt you, and the waves come and the waves erase it.

**

Conversations you can't participate in.

Piles of overdue books.

Keychains without working flashlights.

The line of ants looks like a crack in the wall.

To write on one's own forearm with the sharp edge of a
bitten-off fingernail.

Supermarket: rice, mustard, toothpaste, Scotch tape,
acetominophen.

Jorge (jardinero): 224 5678

Súper: sal.

Conversaciones en las que no puede participar.

**

Fotos mal centradas
frente a monumentos ecuestres.
El brazo de León Cortés,
la sombra del brazo de León Cortés,
 sobre nuestra biología de 30 años.
Todo, menos los extras de atrás,
parece un montaje en Photoshop.

**

Los hijos de la Segunda República
reprodujéronse a lo que venga,
alimentaron a estos que se afeitan
la cabeza, el pecho, las axilas.
Secretamente saben que es el 2 de agosto
el Día de la Independencia.

**

Cada cuatro meses,
cual inspector fiscal,
la madre pregunta si es adicto.

Jorge (the gardener): 224-5678.

Supermarket: salt.

Conversations you can't participate in.

**

Off-center photographs
in front of equestrian monuments.
Leon Cortes's arm,
the shadow of Leon Cortes's arm,
cast on the biology of thirty year-olds.
Apart from the extras behind us, everything
looks like a Photoshopped montage.

**

The children of the Second Republic
reproduced without
thinking, fed those who shaved
heads and chests and armpits.
Secretly they know it's August 2nd
Independence Day.

**

Every four months,
like a tax auditor,
his mother asks if he is an addict.

**

Diusgaurdi, piensa.
Diusguardi, dice.

**

Fotos mal enfocadas,
fotos de la gente
que consume ansiolíticos
envueltos en papel de golosina
mientras ve películas mal dobladas.
Una tarde, un cine de provincia,
tanda para desempleados.

**

Tengo esas fotos que antes tuvimos.
Si superponemos los rostros
aparece Linda Blair,
aparece aquel travesti
que conocemos desde la primaria.

**

En el lugar del corazón,
una piedra con la forma
de la Virgen criolla
que nos liberó de los españoles,
de tu mamá, tus hermanos, del sobrepeso,
de comprender el misterio de la Trinidad.

**

May God keep you, she thinks.
Bless, she says.

**

Out-of-focus photographs,
photographs of people
who consume anxiolytics
rolled-up in a candy wrapper
while they watch badly dubbed films.
One afternoon, a cinema in the suburbs,
a screening for the unemployed.

**

I have these photographs that used to be ours.
If we superimpose the faces,
Linda Blair appears,
that drag queen appears,
the one we've known since elementary school.

**

In place of the heart,
a stone in the shape
of La Virgen Criolla
who liberated us from the Spanish,
from your mother, from your brothers, from fatness,
from understanding the mystery of the Trinity.

**

En la orilla del Pacífico
miráamos atentos el fuego
como si fuera un tele inteligente.

Los brillos del gel en tu cabeza
eran estrellas mortales, diminutas,
extinguiéndose.

**

Podría ser peor,
así llegamos a los 40.
Pronto se despejará la bruma,
Dios mediante,
para tomarnos la foto de grupo, de país,
para empezar donde se detuvo el cojo.

**

Fotos mal centradas
cada cuatro meses,
billetes defectuosos
en el bolsillo del pantalón,
el sol visto desde un planeta plano,
los pericos de aquel mes
cuando bajamos los brazos
creyendo que los subíamos.

**

On the coast of the Pacific
we'd watch the fire attentively
as if it were an intelligent TV.

The glitter of gel in your hair
was a host of mortal stars, diminutive,
extinguishing themselves.

**

It could be worse.
This is how we arrive at our 40s.
By the grace of God,
the fog will soon disperse,
so that we can take a photograph of the group, of the
country,
so that we can begin where the man with the limp left
off.

**

Off-center photographs
every four months,
defective bills
in a pants pocket,
the sun as seen from a flat planet,
the parakeets that month
when we lowered our arms
believing we were raising them.

Part TWO

EQUESTRIAN MONUMENTS

AFUERA DEL AGUA

(A Partir de "Abajo Del Agua" de S. Llach)

1.

El Pacífico visto desde la Interamericana, de noche, detrás de la ventanilla de un bus repleto de desconocidos, rumbo a Dominical. En eso pienso. Es una imagen sin duda ordinaria pero que no me abandona. Una imagen arbitraria, que regresa cada tanto, igual que esas olas que adivino deshaciéndose en la arena, devolviendo ramas, caracoles, una chancleta, corchos, tetrabriks vacíos, como boyas de la decadencia encallando de nuevo en el continente. El mar visto de noche, cuando es invisible y habla en ese lenguaje oscuro y poderoso, para que sepamos que está ahí, donde los ojos no sirven. El mar de noche, más profundo y temible que de día. El mar de las canciones simples, los ahogados y los peces.

Más atrás en el tiempo, la misma noche, el mismo mar, la misma arena en la que sentados, sin hablar, hundíamos los pies hasta los tobillos, hipnotizados por el fuego y el baile de las pavesas que se elevaban hasta desaparecer en el aire con chasquidos mudos. Alguien, alejándose, escuchaba en la radio noticias de un mundo que parecía suspenderse a millones de años luz de aquel lugar, de aquel momento. Otros, acercándose y cruzando detrás de nuestras espaldas, extendían una conversación que bien podría haber sido nuestra. Y también, sí, el ladrido en cadena de los perros, las luces de las casas apagándose una a una.

OUT OF WATER

(After "Abajo del Agua" by S. Llach)

1.

The Pacific Ocean at night, seen from inside a bus full of strangers en route to Dominical by way of the Interamerican highway. This is what I'm thinking about now. It's an ordinary image without a doubt, but (for some reason) it won't leave me alone. An arbitrary vision that comes back every now and again, same as those waves I can almost see unmaking themselves in the sand; branches, seashells, a sandal, corks, and wine cartons brought back like buoys from some other ruin run aground on a new continent. The sea at night, when it's invisible. When it speaks in tongues, so that we know it's still there, where sight doesn't serve us. The night's sea, lonelier and even less fathomable than the day's. The sea of simpler songs only the drowned and the fish know to sing.

Earlier the same night, the same sea, the same sand where, without a word, we'd bury our feet up to the ankles, rapt by the fire and the embers, dervishing until they disappear with a crackling in the air only half-heard. Not so far away, someone is listening to the radio, listening to news of a world that may as well have been suspended a million light years from what is here now. Others come up close behind us. We overhear a conversation that could have been an extension of our own. And yes, the dogs barking in back yards, all the house lights going out one by one.

2.

¿Por qué, una noche cualquiera, en un sueño aparece
en vestido de baño la exnovia de cuarto año del colegio
de quien no tenemos noticias desde la graduación? ¿Por
qué de pronto, digamos un jueves, enfrascado en tareas
cotidianas, uno daría el pulgar derecho por volver a la
mañana del 1º de enero en que se amaneció en la banca
de un parquecito deprimente de playa Dominical, frente
a un mar nada amistoso, averiado, sin plata para el bus
de regreso, rodeado de los cuerpos todavía tendidos de
subnormales con quienes la noche anterior, abrazados
y a los gritos, se juró amistad eterna? El mar no nos lo
explica. Ni le importa.

La orilla del mar contaminado por la fauna de
las vacaciones, el fondo del mar moviéndose al ritmo
imperceptible del combustible fósil. Pescadores, mar
adentro, meando desde cubierta. Cetáceos menores y
gaviotas escoltando a los barcos de hombres solos.

Los que cierran los ojos para hacer promesas falsas
frente al mar. Los que no los cierran. Los que creen
que basta mojarse los pies en el mar para conocer sus
profundidades.

Los que construyen castillos de arena, los que
se dejan enterrar en ella. Los que, eructando, lanzan
botellas al mar, sin mensajes. Los que intuyen que el
mar no es más que un montón de agua.

En el álbum familiar, el espacio vacío, rectangular,
de la foto perdida del niño con tendencia a la obesidad,

2.

Why, on this particular night, does an ex-girlfriend from your senior year in high school show up in a dream wearing nothing but a swimsuit, when you've not heard from her since graduation?

On a Thursday, say, running the same errands you'd run any other day, why are you suddenly willing to give one of your thumbs to go back to the bench you woke-up on, in a depressing little park outside of Dominical on New Year's Day? That morning, destroyed, having to face a standoffish ocean, no money for the bus, bodies all around, asleep; they are lying there still, the deviants you swore you'd love forever, arms around each other's necks last night, howling. The sea does not explain. The sea does not care to, not to us anyway.

An over-population of fauna on the shore, the vacationing kind. The sea, where it's deepest, moving to the imperceptible rhythm of fossil fuel. Fishermen, further in, pissing covertly. Seagulls and small aquatic mammals escort boats travelling with only one man aboard.

Those who, facing the ocean, close their eyes and make empty promises. Those who do the same, but don't close their eyes. Those who stand in ankle-deep water, believing the whole ocean's knowable from that depth. Those who let themselves be buried in the sand, those who build sandcastles. Those who pitch messageless bottles into the ocean, belching. Those who intuit the ocean is no more than a whole lot of water.

In the family album, an empty space, a rectangle: lost photograph of the boy with a tendency towards

sólo en la playa, de pie frente al Pacífico, una mañana limpia del 74. Aquella en la que, en ángulo recto, su figura y su sombra leve sobre la arena formaban un reloj de sol. El mar como una golosina.

fearing fatness, alone on the beach, standing in front of the Pacific, the cleanest morning in 1974. That morning, at a right angle, his figure and the slight shadow he casts over the sand forms a sundial. The sea like hard candy.

UN FERIADO
NO OBLIGATORIO

(Fragmentos de un Primer Borrador)

Hoy nos levantamos con los primeros ruidos de la mañana, nada literarios por cierto: el desfile de aplanadoras y vagonetas escoltadas por una tropilla de obreros. La procesión de la santa obra pública. Cuando desperté, le comprabas un foco al coreano que atendía detrás de un mostrador. El mostrador era el mismo de la pulpería de Tulio pero en el sueño era del coreano que te vendía el foco que, aclaraba, era "sumelgible".

En el piso de arriba, la estudiante de canto empezó sus ejercicios matinales una hora más tarde. Esta mañana no repasó la melodía que se parece a la canción aquella de la que sólo recuerdo el estribillo. En el techo del edificio de enfrente, toma sol la hija del vecino sobre un paño que no le llega a los tobillos. Tiene algodones blancos sobre los pezones. Se los cambia. Tiene pezones purpúreos bajo los algodones blancos.

Anoche volvías tarde o más bien temprano. Te quitaste la ropa de espalda al espejo y mitad dormido, mitad queriendo estarlo, vi cómo de tus calzones caía confeti. Hoy nos levantamos, ya fue dicho, con los primeros ruidos de lo único que podemos definir como progreso. Cuando salíamos, sentada contra bolsas de cemento, la mano de obra extranjera tomaba café con leche en botellas de Coca-Cola.

ON A HOLIDAY NOT EVERYONE'S OBSERVING

(Fragments of a First Draft)

Today we woke up to the first few sounds of morning. Nothing literary about them: a parade of bulldozers and dump trucks escorted by platoons of workers. A holy procession of public works. I woke up the moment you were buying a flashlight from a Korean man, the one with the slight stutter, standing behind a counter, the same as the one at Tulio's corner store, but in the dream it belonged to the cashier who insisted that the flashlight would work underwater.

The music student upstairs began her morning voice exercises an hour later than usual. This morning she didn't rehearse the one melody that reminds me of that song I only know the chorus from. On a roof deck across the street, the neighbor's daughter is sunbathing on a towel that's barely ankle-length. She covers each nipple with a cotton ball, which she replaces often. She has purplish nipples beneath the cotton.

You were coming home late last night—rather, you were coming home early. You undressed with your back to the mirror, and, half asleep, half wanting to be asleep entirely, I saw the confetti fall from your panties. Like I said before, today we woke up to the first few sounds of the only thing we can properly call "progress." On our way out, we saw migrant workers leaning against bags of cement, drinking their café con leche from Coca-Cola bottles.

Qué querrías hacer con un foco sumergible, me pregunto mientras termino la tercera vuelta al parque La Sabana. Entretanto, el parque es invadido por grupos de familias que avanzan a la velocidad de la frontera agrícola. Van dejando señales de basura inorgánica para luego reconocer el camino de regreso a sus hogares. Es la quinta vuelta y te saludo, allá tirada sobre el mantel a cuadros, bajo la sombra que proyectan unos pinos moribundos, con la ropa que no te cambiás desde anteayer, leyendo la novela cuyo narrador —dando en el clavo ya en 1932— afirma que hay algo más importante que el amor: la belleza, la belleza física.

La maleza crece cuando dejamos de mirar. Los años se acumulan mientras nos ocupamos de la maleza. Aprender esto nos tomó más tiempo del que hubiéramos querido. Ahora se encienden los faroles del alumbrado municipal, de los carros que pasan con las ventanas abiertas. En el parque, dos hermanos, aferrados al juego, se esfuerzan por seguir la trayectoria de un balón que empieza a pertenecer a la noche.

Es la hora de volver, para no extraviarnos seguimos el rastro de basura de los vecinos. Caminamos juntos. A esta altura del partido, tomarnos de las manos es un acto mental. Del día nos quedaremos con fotos mal enfocadas frente a monumentos ecuestres, con el eco decreciente de un sueño menos extraño que inútil, con el estribillo de la canción que escapa de un carro en movimiento y que no dejaremos de tararear el resto de la semana.

What could you have wanted an underwater flashlight for, I ask myself, my third time around La Sabana. Meanwhile, the park is invaded by tour groups, families advancing at the speed of deforestation. Behind them, they leave a trail of things that'll never biodegrade to find their way back home later on. It's my fifth lap around the park, I see you and say hello. Lying on the tablecloth, the checkered one, in the shade of dying pine trees, you're wearing the same clothes from the day before yesterday, reading the novel whose narrator— in 1932, mind you—suggests there's something more important than love: nature, beauty, natural beauty.

The weeds grow when we stop watching them. The years accumulate while we worry about the weeds. Learning this took longer than we would have liked. The municipality's streetlights come on one by one now, so do the lights of cars driving by with their windows down. In the park, with undivided attention on the game they play, two brothers struggle to follow the trajectory of a ball that they'll soon lose to the night.

It's time to go back. We follow the trail of plastic so we don't lose our way. We walk together. This late in the game, to take one another by the hand is an act of will. By day, we're left with out-of-focus photographs in front of equestrian monuments, the fading echo of a dream less strange than it is useless, the chorus of a song overheard from a passing car. And we won't stop humming for the rest of the week.

INVENTARIO

Había clips; monedas de diez y cinco céntimos; cabos de borradores Staedtler, también dos imitaciones made-in-china de borradores Staedtler; entradas para cines y películas diversas de épocas asimismo diversas (destaca la de King Kong en el cine Caribe de Zapote, desaparecido en la última era glacial); disquetes con marbetes nada comprometidos estilo "varios", o tautológicos tipo "documentos"; un anuncio de periódico con la leyenda "Do you have a cocaine problem?", envío de una amiga que se llevó su chispa y buen humor a otro país; un llavero con el escudo del Club Sport Herediano (pasión familiar transmitida de generación en generación junto con la promesa del cáncer gástrico); varias cajas de fósforos: una de hotel sudaca de Barcelona, otra de bar modernoso de San Francisco y la clásica con perforación en el cráter del volcán Arenal; poemas de poetas border sólo publicados en la Web; mi primera cédula de identidad; mi última licencia de conducir; un Durex vencido (sí, ese); varias Voltarén vencidas también; números viejos de Los amigos de lo ajeno; ¡¡¡un floppy!!! (ese fósil de la informática); posavasos con la heráldica de cervezas nacionales y extranjeras; un lápiz Mongol 2 consumido casi hasta el borrador; libretas con frases

INVENTORY

There were paper clips; nickels and dimes; stubs of a few Staedtlers; also two off-brand erasers MADE IN CHINA which look a lot like Staedtlers; tickets to different movies at different movie houses from very different periods (like the Caribe de Zapote where *King Kong* premiered, before the theatre disappeared an ice age ago); floppy disks (diskettes?) with labels that implicate nothing and no one ("miscellaneous," for example), or tautologies (as in, "documents"); an ad from a magazine with the caption "Do you have a cocaine problem?", sent from a friend who decided to take all her mischievousness to another country; a keychain with Club Sport Herediano's logo (love for this team is a family tradition passed from generation to generation, along with a predisposition to stomach cancer); random match boxes: one from Barcelona's South American hotel, another from an ultra-modern bar in San Francisco and a third one, a classic, with a hole where you'd expect to see the crater of Arenal's volcano; poems by emerging poets which were only published online); my first ID card; my last driver's license; an expired Durex (yes, that one); a dose of Voltaren (also expired) and a handful of other anti-inflammatories; back issues of our zine *Los Amigos de lo Ajeno;* ¡¡¡a floppy disk!!! (that fossil of information technology); coasters embossed with the brand names of beers, domestic and imported; a pencil, a Mongol, a #2, used down almost to the eraser; notebooks full of

que supongo valoré célebres en el momento y estado en que las redacté; otras libretas con listas de palabras y latinismos para buscar en ese diccionario que está a la par de los propósitos de Año Nuevo; una caja de grapas; una polaroid tomada en aquella noche de veinticuatro meses que empezó en Las Ventanas y terminó en Regina 51; la fotocopia del pasaje de un ensayo con el término "oxímoron" encerrado en un círculo; un viejo cassette visiblemente carreteado, con una selección de canciones sin duda bien meditada: el lado A como banda sonora para días de sol y filantropía, el lado B (romántico- depre sin fisuras) como la aplanadora que prepara la autopista hacia el suicidio; mapas de ciudades en las que todo funciona; agendas telefónicas de años inverosímiles como 1983; otras agendas telefónicas donde hay nombres y números tachados con el Papermate de la venganza; el recorte de la necrológica de uno que apenas conocí, muerto en accidente de tránsito hace más de doce años; tres encendedores con el logo de La Tortuguita del 96; cartas de gente que ya no conozco; cartas de gente que nunca llegué a conocer; cartas de gente de la que me encantaría seguir recibiendo cartas; esa foto de grupo donde casi parece cierto que nos unía la amistad; esa otro foto frente al monumento ecuestre donde seguimos envejeciendo; un dado solo; esa envoltura de golosina infalible: cada vez que la veo vuelven la luz, los sonidos, el olor del lugar donde la recibí; un pedazo de papel con la frase "tengo fotos que antes tuvimos" garabateada con marcador rojo; un anillo, un juego de aretes, una pulsera, que no son un anillo, un juego de aretes, una

lines and phrases I must've been really taken by when I was writing them down, given the state of mind I was in at the time; other notebooks with lists of words and colloquialisms to look up in the dictionary alongside my New Year's resolutions; a box of staples; a polaroid taken that night that began at Las Ventanas and ended, twenty four months later, at Regina 51; a photocopy of an essay, one part in particular where the term "oxymoron" is circled; an old cassette tape I must have lugged everywhere, with a selection of songs which were well chosen, to say the least: side A, a soundtrack for days of sun and altruism; side B (emo without apology) like a steamroller flattening the freeway that leads to suicide; maps of cities where everything works as it should; address books from years as hard to believe as 1983; other address books with names and numbers that have been vengefully redacted with White Out; a clipping of the obituary belonging to someone I barely knew, who died in a car accident more than twelve years ago; three lighters with La Tortuguita's logo circa 1996; letters from people I don't know anymore; letters from people I never got the chance to know; letters from people I'd love to keep getting letters from; that photo of the group where the friendship between us seems almost certain; that other photo, taken in the same place, in front of the same equestrian monument, evidence that we keep getting older and older; a single die; the indelible candy wrapper: everything comes back every time I see it, the light, the sounds, the smell of the place where it was first unwrapped; a piece of paper with the phrase "I have photos that used to be ours" scribbled in red marker; a

pulsera; una hoja totalmente en blanco salvo por el encabezado interrumpido: Querida _____

ring, a pair of earrings, a bracelet that isn't a ring, a pair of earrings, or a bracelet; a single page completely blank except for the broken salutation: Dear_____.

FALSO DOCUMENTAL

(A Partir de "Esta Es La Nueva Canción de la Que Te Hablé Hace 20 Años," de BDB)

En la tele pasan un caballo que habla nuestro idioma. En la radio a un hombre que habla el idioma de los caballos. Lo cierto sucede en otra parte. El sol está quieto en un cielo sin nubes. Al balcón llegan pájaros a comer las migas de pan que tiré horas antes para que vinieran a alegrarme la mañana. Se acercan primero con timidez, picotean el suelo, me miran de costado, luego vuelan a otro balcón. No podría ser una parábola más pobre, pero me hacen pensar en algo que nada tiene que ver con la alegría.

El polvo avanza en el comedor como una enfermedad o una bendición, dependiendo de quien lo mire. Si sé que ese fenómeno lo explica la física, ¿por qué la sospecha de una fuerza sobrenatural? El día no ofrece más opción que un paneo lento sobre estos últimos años. Ahí están los restos y desechos que dejó la marea de una época convulsa. Unos sobre otros, confundidos los inicios con los desenlaces, los intentos de reanudación con los fracasos. De pronto, el viento cambia de dirección y abajo, en la calle, un conductor reacciona a la luz verde del semáforo. Y aunque estoy consciente de ser discípulo del error, lo interpreto como una señal, como si el universo girara en torno a mí.

FALSE DOCUMENTARY

(After "Esta Es La Nueva Canción De La Que Te Hablé Hace 20 Años" by BDB)

On TV there's a horse. It is speaking our language. On the radio, there's a man speaking the language of horses. What is real must be happening somewhere else. For a second, the sun is still in a cloudless sky. A few hours ago I scattered breadcrumbs for the birds on the balcony, so they would come in the morning. They bring me such joy; they come closer, timidly at first, pecking at the ground, giving me sidelong glances before flying off to another balcony. There couldn't be a sadder parabola. Makes me think of something that has nothing to do with joy.

Dust spreads through the dining room with the stealth of a sickness or a blessing, depending on who you ask. Yes, I know physics can explain this phenomenon—why suspect the supernatural is at work? Other than a slow pan over the last few years, the day doesn't give us any other option. There is the debris a tide washed up in a violent convulsion. One thing after the other, the beginnings and the endings confused. Confusing our attempts at reconciliation with our failures to be reconciled. All of a sudden, a shift in the wind's direction and below, at street-level, a driver responds as the light changes from red to green. And even though I am wrong all the time—I am error's own disciple—I am interpreting this as a sign. As if the universe revolved around me.

Repito mentalmente la letra de una canción que aprendí mal. Es probable que recuerde cosas que no dice. Solemos pensar que una canción es buena si habla de nosotros. Debe ser que todas las vidas se parecen. Si es así, ¿qué será de esa niña, allá en la otra acera, que no sabe si comer el helado que se le derrite o si acariciar al perro que salta a su lado moviendo la cola?

Antes de darlo por finalizado apenas en septiembre, creí que el 2004 sería un buen año. Ahora la casa es una bolsa con ropa sucia en mitad de la sala, dos o tres novelas abandonadas antes del final, los boletos de un viaje en ferry, un mensaje en el contestador donde aquella voz pregunta por los planes de un viernes ya lejano. Es así, todo período se puede reducir a una simple enumeración.

Quería explicarte otra cosa, pero la voluntad es engañosa como los espejos de los gimnasios. Y sin embargo, quizás está bien quedarse en el balcón, sin pájaros, observar desde arriba lo que dentro de unas horas me superará. Está bien seguir con la vista la ruta de la equivocación. En algún lugar están las personas que fuimos, un espacio donde la prueba y el error se repiten una y otra vez, con una canción de fondo que dice lo que queremos escuchar.

Pero el lugar que importa es éste. Las hojas de los árboles se mecen con el viento norte y con el humo del progreso. Sostenida por un imán, en la puerta del refrigerador, está la foto que tomaste la noche en que un ciclo terminaba mucho antes de que lo supiéramos.

The lyrics of a song I must have misheard are stuck in my head. It's likely I'm only remembering parts that were never there to begin with. We tend to think a song is good if it seems to be about us. Everyone must lead very similar lives. If that's true, what to make of that girl on the sidewalk who doesn't know whether to eat the ice cream melting down her wrist or pet the dog jumping alongside her, wagging its tail.

Before making my mind up sometime in September, I believed 2004 was going to be a good year. Now the house is a bag full of dirty clothes in the middle of the living room, two or three novels abandoned before I could finish them, ferry tickets, a message on the answering machine, that voice asking me about plans for last Friday or the one before that. This is how it is. A whole period of time can be condensed into a simple inventory.

I meant to explain something else to you, but the will is misleading like those mirrors at the gym. And yet, maybe it's ok to stay up here on the balcony, without any birds, to see what, within a few hours, will overcome me. It's OK to re-visit where I went wrong, to see it with my own eyes. The people we used to be are in a place where trial and error seem to repeat themselves again and again, while a song in the background tells us exactly what we want to hear.

But this is the only place that matters. The leaves yield to the north wind and the smog of progress. On the refrigerator, held-up by a magnet, is the photo you took the night one of our phases ended well before we thought it would.

Esto lo escribo una mañana luminosa. Entre los edificios de enfrente, cerca de la avenida Córdoba, pasa un avión. Cruza el cielo en silencio, en cámara lenta, como impulsado por el motor del recuerdo. La vida de afuera parece fluir con calma y naturalidad. Quiero que la vida de adentro también.

I am writing this on a light-filled morning. I can see a plane between the buildings across the way, the ones facing Avenida Cordoba. It cuts across the sky in silence, in slow-motion, as if its engines were fueled by memory. The outside world seems to flow with naturalness and calm. I want the inside world that way too.

EQUESTRIAN MONUMENTS

ACKNOWLEDGEMENTS

The translators would like to thank editors of the following magazines where some of this work has previously appeared or will soon be forthcoming (sometimes in slightly different form): Boston Review, Circumference, The Guardian, Guernica, PEN Poetry Series, Springhouse and POETRY.

Special gratitude to The Poetry Foundation for awarding our translation of the title poem, "Equestrian Monuments," the John Frederic Nims Memorial Prize in Translation.

The translators dedicate "Wyoming" to Iris Cushing.

ACKNOWLEDGEMENTS
from JULIA GUEZ

Thank you to Rosa Carballo Venegas at Good Light Books, where all of this began. Thank you to Jose Gonzalez Ugalde, Carlos Francisco Monge, Jonatan Lepiz Vega, Harris Schiff, Juan Antillón and Adriano Corrales Arias for grounding me in the wonderful work happening in workshops, festivals and presses in San José. Thank you to Mary Ann Stark and *The Tico Times* for profiling my work as a Fulbright Fellow. Thank you to Jessica Mehta, for the introduction that soon followed that piece. Thank you to Luis Chaves and María José Gavilan for the pleasure of walking this way together, ever since that introduction all those years ago. Thank you to Andrea Mickus and Gustavo Chaves for your own work as writers, translators and curators; thank you both for founding Libreria Duluoz; thank you for hosting the kind of dinner parties where projects like this one might be born.

Thank you to El Taller Literario Alajuelense (David Monge and Bernabé Berrocal, in particular). Thank you to The Fulbright Commission; thank you, in particular, to Jody Dudderar and Pamela Jennings for supporting me throughout my research in Costa Rica. Thank you to the United States Embassy in San José; thank you, in particular, to Oscar Avila and Sue Lyn Erbeck; your friendship has meant the world to us.

Thank you to Richard Howard, Stefania Heim, Idra Novey and Susan Bernofsky; thank you to everyone working to support Literary Translation at Columbia. Thank you to Ricardo Maldonado for your friendship, for your poetry and, also, for the magic in that *Nocturno*. Thank you to Mary Jo Bang for your genius and innovation as a translator and for your close and careful read of this translation (which is so much stronger because of your notes).

Thank you to my teachers and my students.

Thank you, again, to Edith Grossman. What an honor to call you my mentor and friend. Thank you to María Montero. Thank you for your art, for your example, and for your friendship over the years. Thank you, again, to Ori Braun (and thank you to the entire Braun, Stocker and Shirley clan). You are family to us now; the peninsula is home.

Thank you to Samantha Zighelboim, for the joy of translating this collection together, for your friendship throughout the years of its making (and for the many meals and conversations, films, drinks and retreats this collaboration would entail). Grateful, in particular, for our time on The North Fork and the light we found at Goldsmith's Inlet, the sea like hard candy there.

Many thanks to everyone at After Hours Editions, especially Sarah Jean Grimm and Eric Amling; grateful for your vision, grateful for your attention to every detail, grateful for your many kindnesses.

Thank you to all of the editors whose support gave this project life along the way. Thank you, in particular, to Don Share, Liz Clark Wessel, Iris Cushing, Joshua Daniel Edwin, Danniel Schoonnebeek, Timothy Donnelly, Tomás Cohen, Erica Wright and Soren Stockman.

Thanks, finally, to my family here and abroad. My work with translation began at home, at our dinner table. Thanks to my mother and father, my brothers, my aunts, uncles and cousins, my niece and my nephews. Thanks, also, to my mother-in-law, my father-in-law, my brother-in-law and my sisters-in-law. And thanks, most of all, to my wife and sons. None of this would be possible without you. So grateful for the light you bring every sky. I am over all the moons to get to love the likes of you, my Little Dipper, my Big Dipper and, of course, our North Star.

ACKNOWLEDGEMENTS
from SAMANTHA ZIGHELBOIM

To the Dream Team: Love and gratitude to my friend and co-conspirator, Julia Guez, who eight years ago invited me to be part of this project. For this leap of faith you took with me, the yerba mates and cortaditos and amaros, the long afternoons of translating that always ended in family dinners, the dreaming and scheming over warm spicy scallop handrolls and sake, the less glamorous moments we had the good fortune of laughing and crying through together, and for the joy and friendship we cultivated from The East Village to Greenpoint to Murray Hill to the North Fork of Long Island and back—I am eternally grateful, my friend. To the inimitable Luis Chaves, for trusting us with this extraordinary collection, and giving us the creative freedom to bring it to English-reading audiences. Love & rockets.

Deeply grateful to Eric Amling & Sarah Jean Grimm at After Hours Editions, for loving these poems as much as we do, and making them such a beautiful home.

Thanks to Edith Grossman, Mary Jo Bang, Charif Shanahan, and Ricardo Maldonado, for your beautiful words about the book, and your invaluable insight and guidance.

Love and gratitude to the friends and chosen family who have held me up and cheered on this work from its inception: Alexis Baldwin, Danny Bravo, Samantha Charlip, Iris Cushing, Tiffany Kallhovd, Simone Kearney, Dorothea Lasky, Ricardo Maldonado (again y por siempre), Ali Power, Katie Raissian, Eliza Schrader, Jimin Seo, Emily Skillings, Liz Clark Wessel, and Eric Dean Wilson.

To my beloved teachers and mentors, Timothy Donnelly, Lucie Brock-Broido and Jen Bervin; with special thanks to the one and only Richard Howard, who has yet to see this collection at the time I am writing this, but who has categorically shaped who I am as a translator and poet, both with his own work and his friendship over the years.

And finally, endless thanks to my family, especially Sonia Zighelboim, Daniel Z. Daum, Ann Dai, Manuel Fihman, and Katia Yurguis. Y para la Nena, quien siempre me corrigió el español, y quien en sus últimos días se contentó mucho en saber las noticias sobre la publicación de este libro.

ABOUT THE AUTHOR
AND TRANSLATORS

Luis Chaves (San José, 1969) is considered one of the most important contemporary authors in Costa Rica. He has written poetry, fiction and non-fiction. He has published, among others, the poetry books *Los animales que imaginamos* (1997), *Chan Marshall* (2005) and the anthology *La máquina de hacer niebla* (2012) As well as *300 páginas* (2010, essays), *El Mundial 2010 - apuntes* (2010, chronicles) and *Salvapantallas* (2015, novel). He has been translated into English, German, Dutch, Italian and Slovenian. In 2011 the Akademie Schloss Solitude in Stuttgart awarded him the Jean Jacques Rousseau fellowship and in 2012 he received the National Poetry Award (Costa Rica). In 2015 he was at the DAAD artist residency program in Berlin, and a resident for the Institut for Advanced Studies in Nantes in 2017.. In 2020 his chronicle *Vamos a tocar el agua* was selected as Best Book of the Year by *Rolling Stone* Magazine (Argentina). He lives in Costa Rica.

Julia Guez is a writer and translator based in the city of New York. Her essays, interviews, fiction, poetry and translations have appeared in *Guernica, POETRY, The Guardian, BOMB, The Brooklyn Rail and Kenyon Review*. Four Way Books released her first full-length collection, *In An Invisible Glass Case Which Is Also A*

Frame, in 2019. They will release her next book, *The Certain Body,* in 2022. Guez has been awarded the Discovery/*Boston Review* Poetry Prize, a Fulbright Fellowship and The John Frederick Nims Memorial Prize in Translation as well as a translation fellowship from the National Endowment for the Arts. For the last decade, Guez has worked with Teach For America New York; she's currently the senior managing director of design and implementation. She teaches creative writing at NYU and Rutgers.

Samantha Zighelboim is the author of *The Fat Sonnets* (Argos Books, 2018). She is a 2017 NYFA/NYSCA Fellow in Poetry, a recipient of a Face Out grant from CLMP, and the recipient of the 2016 John Frederick Nims Memorial Prize in Translation from The Poetry Foundation. Her poems, translations and essays appear in *POETRY, Boston Review, Lit Hub, The Guardian, PEN Poetry Series, Guernica, Stonecutter, Fanzine,* and The Poetry Society of America, among others. She teaches creative writing at Columbia University and Parsons School of Design at The New School.